Breathe

athe

Breathe

I Take a DEEEP Breath!

Publisher's Cataloging-in-Publication
(Provided by Quality Books, Inc.)

Penchina, Sharon.
I Take a DEEEP Breath!/ Sharon Penchina and Stuart Hoffman.
p.cm. -- (I am a Lovable Me! ; 2)
SUMMARY: Introduces awareness of breathing as a
self-empowerment tool for children to adopt in order to promote
feelings of well being and as a means to cope with challenges.
Audience: Ages 0-7.
LCCN 2004092702
ISBN 0-9740684-6-2
ISBN 0-9740684-5-4

1. Breathing exercises--Juvenile literature.
2. Respiration--Juvenile literature. 3. Health--Juvenile literature.
[1. Breathing exercises. 2. Respiration. 3. Health. 4.Stories in rhyme.]
1. Hoffman, Stuart, 1957- II. Tile. III. Title: I Take a DEEEP Breath!

RA782.P46 2004   613'.192
QBI33-2034

2imagine

Printed in China

I Take a DEEEP Breath!

By Sharon Penchina C.Ht. & Dr. Stuart Hoffman

For Dale with LOVE!

2 Imagine
Scottsdale, Arizona
United States of America

Proper Breathing is both a Science and an Art

DID YOU KNOW??

- Better breathing keeps you healthy.

- Breathing can calm you.

- Breathing can give you more energy.

- Oxygen is fuel for the body.

- Oxygen feeds your brain so you can think clearly.

- Your body gets oxygen when you breathe in and removes carbon dioxide when you breathe out.

- Oxygen maintains cells. It keeps them clean and healthy.

- Breathing oxygen into the body helps the body fight against illness.

- Breathing into your belly relaxes you.

- Tiny hairs in your nostrils act as filters to purify the air you breathe.

- You can control your breathing and play with your breath.

- Shallow breathing can mean you are stressed out.

- Control your breathing and you manage your emotions.

- The deeper you breathe, the better you feel.

- Being aware of your breathing is the first step to better breathing.

"I Take a DEEEP Breath!"

Part 2 of the "IAM a Lovable ME!"
Self-EMPOWERMENT series
for children and their adults
encourages you to learn the
proper method of breathing.

BREATHING WILL IMPROVE THE QUALITY OF YOUR LIFE!

When I get up in the morning

Lovable Me

I take a deeep breath in and breathe out....

Now I'm ready to try something new,

slowly.......

Like reading a book or tying my shoe.

Now I'm OKAY,

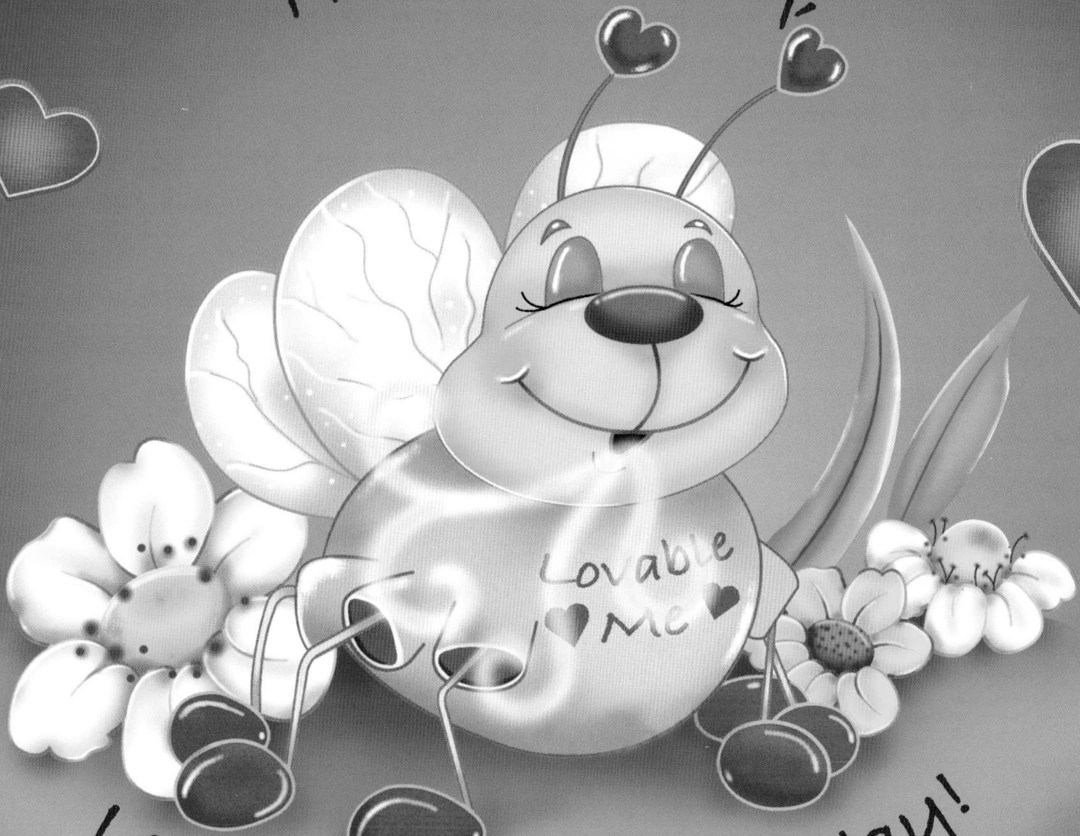

I can get on with my day!

When I meet new friends,

I take a deep breath in and breathe out slowly...

If I feel sad and lonely,

I take a deeep breath in and breathe out slowly....

This helps me feel calm and at ease, safe and sound as I please.

If mom or dad go away

I take a deeep breath in and breathe

out slowly.........

I'm reminded that
they will come back,
there's no need to
keep track.

There are short breaths,

Long breaths,

I'm breathing STRONG breaths.

In breaths, Out breaths, Make you want to SHOUT breaths.

There are quick breaths, Slow breaths, AND GO WITH THE FLOW BREATHS.......

Lovable ♥ Me ♥

There are mouth breaths,
Nose breaths,
Down to your
toes breaths.

There are deep breaths,
Snooze breaths,

Breathe
however you
choose breaths.

BREATHE IN DEEEPLY AND LET IT OUT SLOWLY!

When it's my first day at school,

I take a deeep breath in and breathe out slowly...

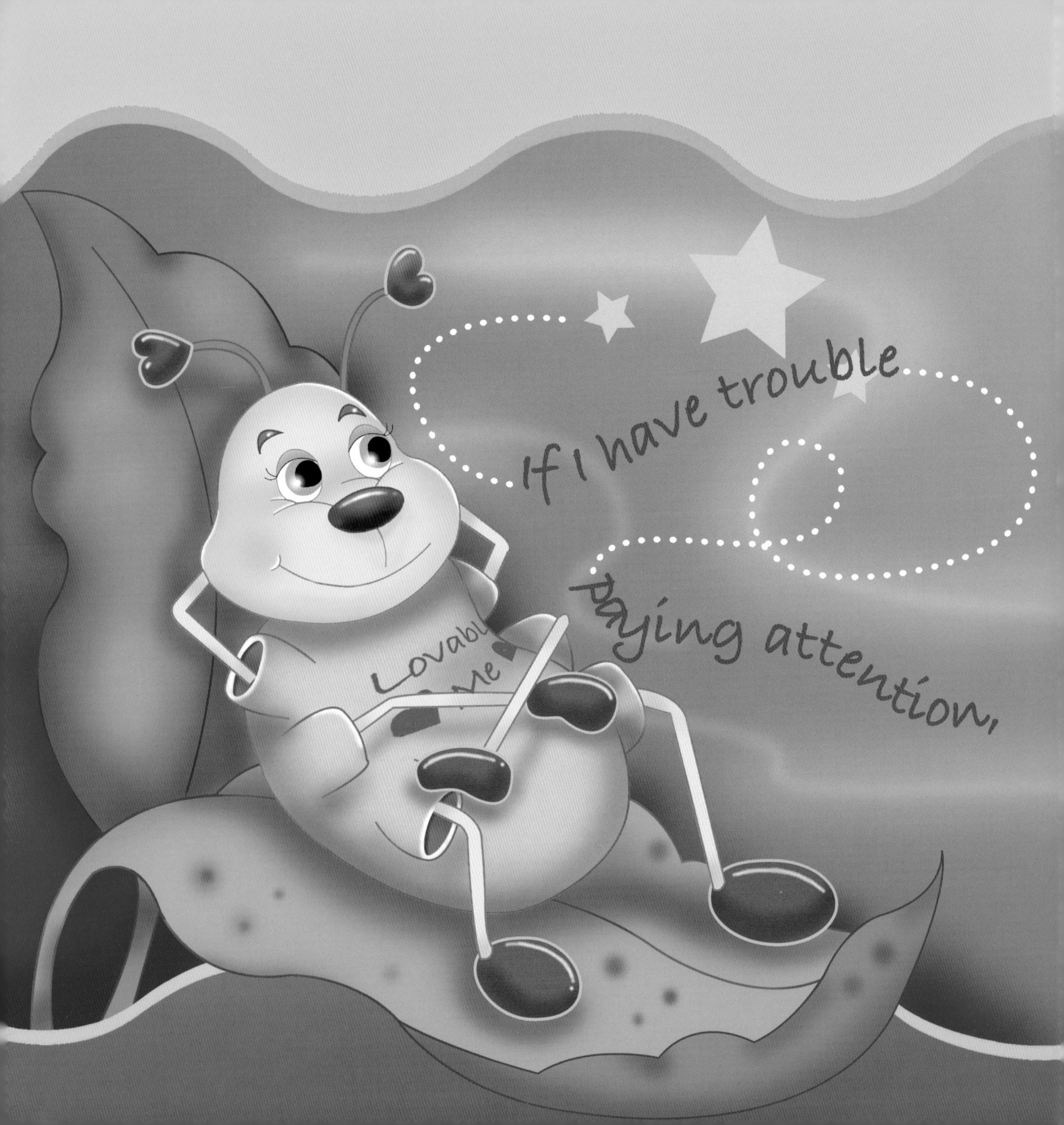

If I have trouble paying attention,

I take a deeep breath in and breathe out slowly...............

This helps me focus, and that's no hocus pocus.

When I run or jump or dance and sing,

I take
a deeep
breath in and
breathe out
slowly....

I can go a lot longer, feeling healthy and stronger.

When I get excited,

I take a deep breath in and breathe out slowly....

There are short breaths, Long breaths, I'm breathing STRONG breaths.

In breaths, Out breaths, Make you want to SHOUT breaths.

Lovable ♥ Me ♥

There are quick breaths, Slow breaths, AND GO WITH THE FLOW BREATHS.......

There are mouth breaths,
Nose breaths,
Down to your
toes breaths.

There are deep breaths,
Snooze breaths,

Breathe
however you
choose breaths.

BREATHE IN DEEEPLY AND LET IT OUT SLOWLY!

If I feel left out by my friends,

I take a deeep breath in and breathe out slowly....

When it's time to clean my room, I take a deeep breath in and breathe out slowly.

Then I take care of my things,

what a good feeling it brings.

If I can't sleep at night,
I take a deeep breath in and breathe
out slowly.....

Now I can fall asleep..... without even a peep.

zzzzzzzzzzzzzzzzzzzz